Adult coloring book
for dog lovers

Copyright © 2019 by Color Joy

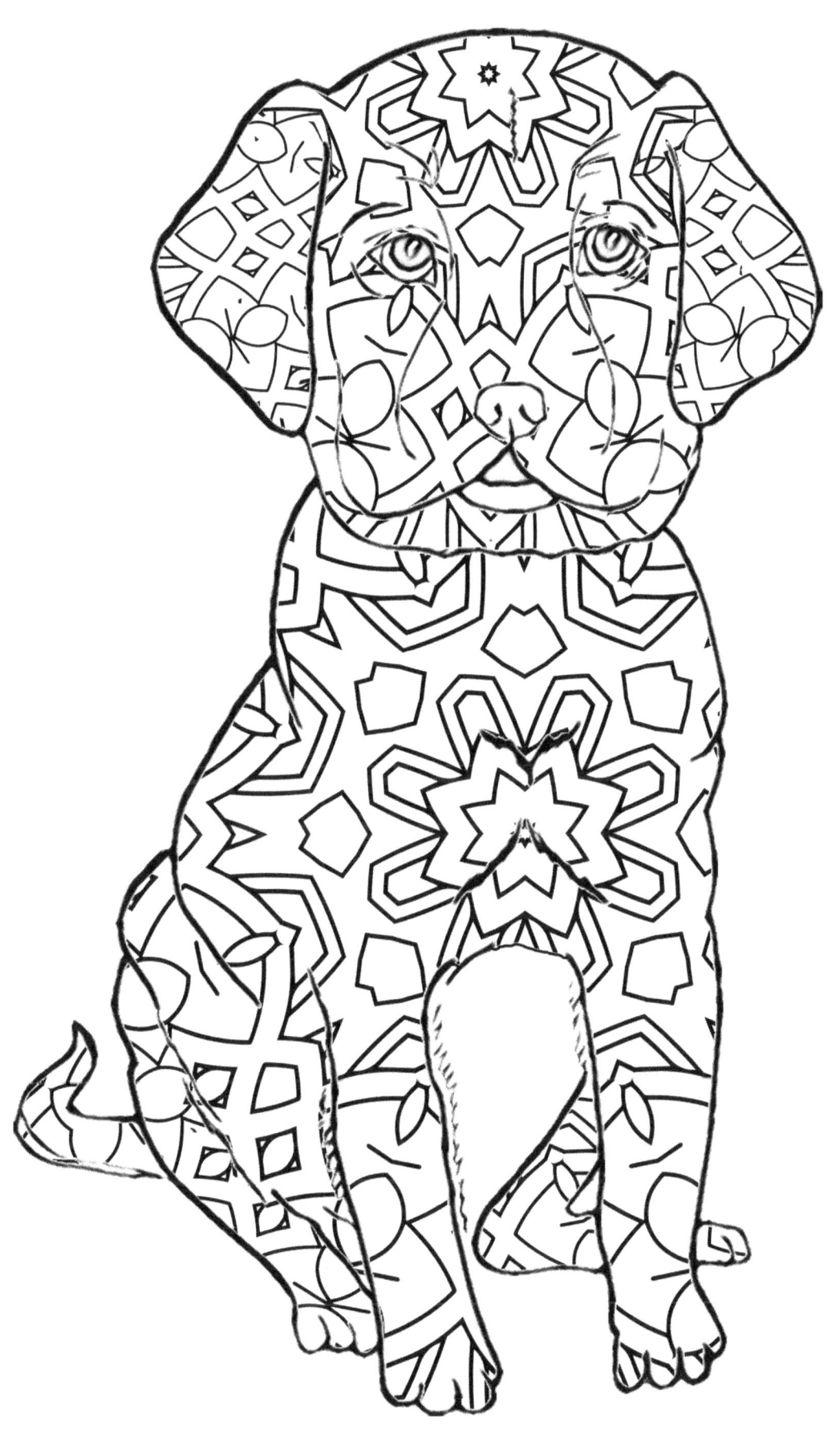

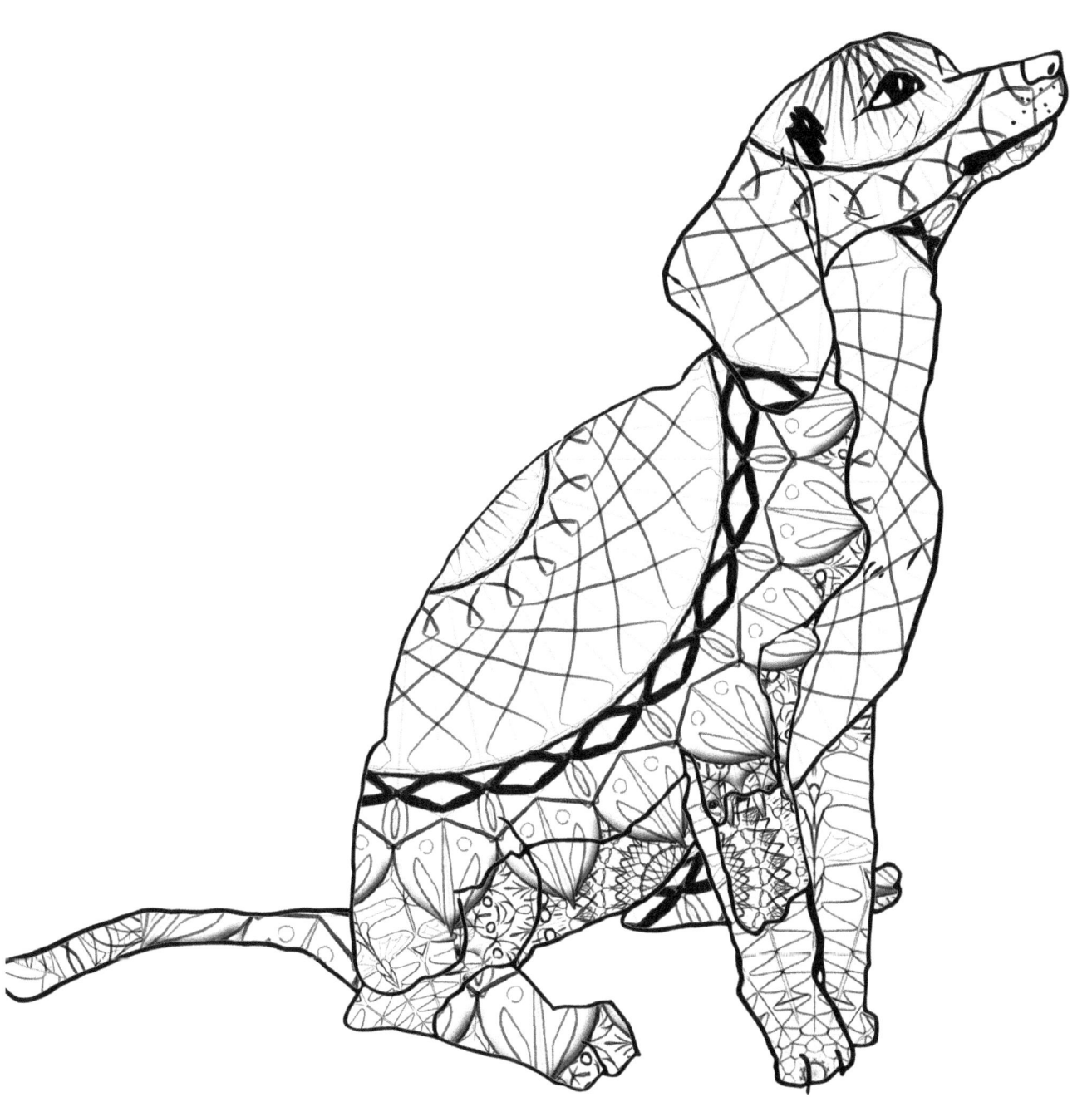

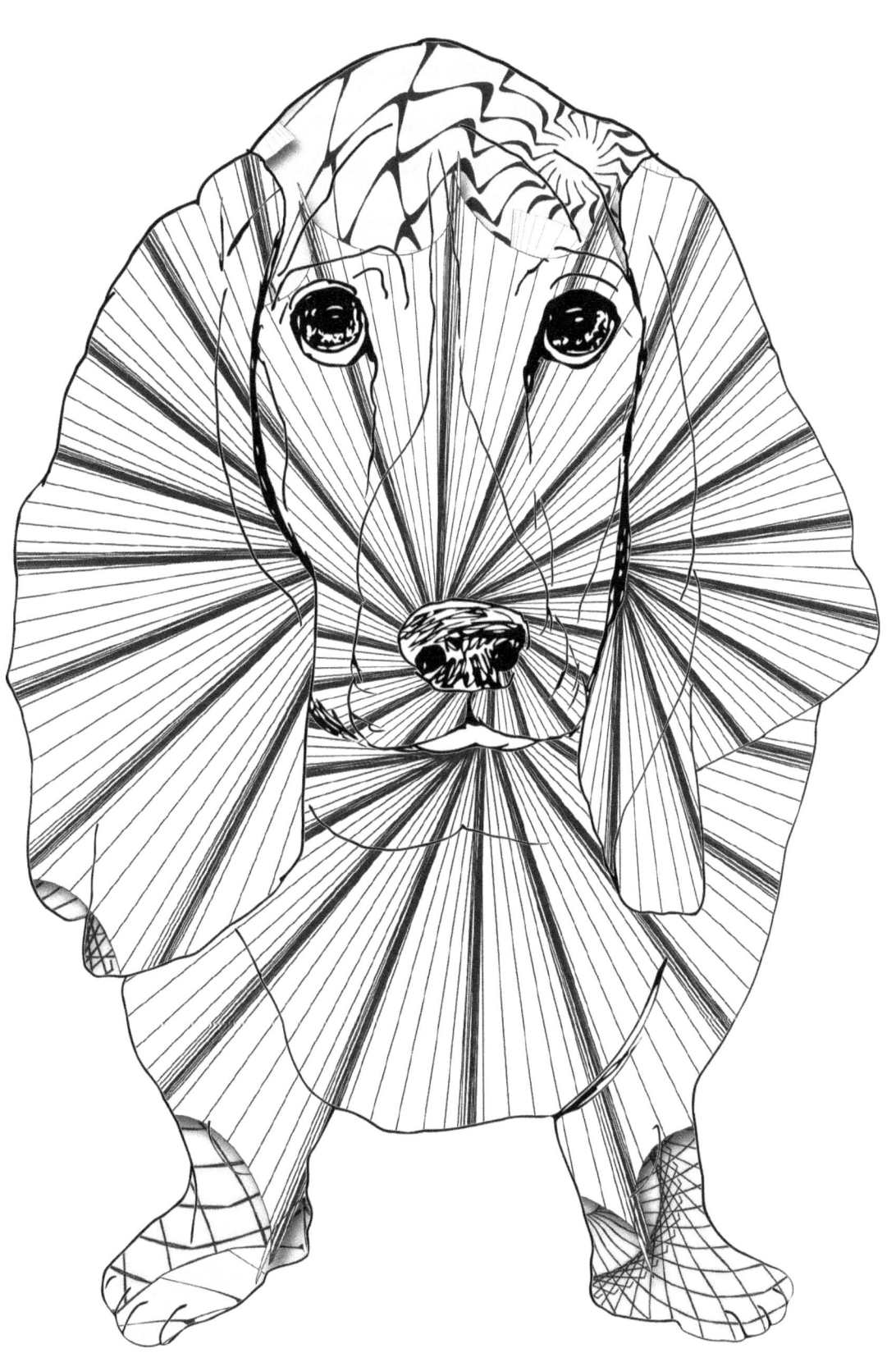

Also by Color Joy:

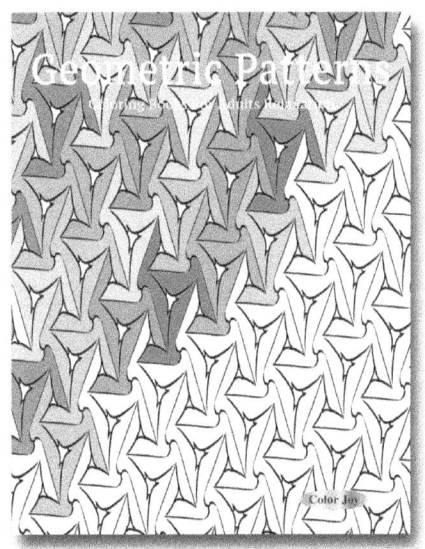

Join us @ Facebook
Twitter
Pinterest

www.ingramcontent.com/pod-product-compliance
Lightning Source LLC
LaVergne TN
LVHW060220080526
838202LV00052B/4311